A Manager's Reflections and
Experiences

Carl B. Pallaver

My good fortune was to be married to a bright, articulate and loving wife. Here's to you my sweet Jeanne.

Contents

FORWARD

I don't have a Ph.D. or a Masters in Management. I am not going to feed to you a massive collection of statistics. I will do my best to make it a fast, easy read and as President Harry Truman used to say "Just plain speaking." What I'm passing on is actual front line experiences from over 40 years of managing people in technical projects costing from thousands to millions of dollars.

My experiences are from a state of the art process technology environment with dangerous gases, massive machines and 24-7 operations in which I hold many patents, have published articles in industry trade magazines and have documented very large process systems.

I offer suggestions on what I believe would make a happy, productive work place. I make no representations regarding the legality of these suggestions. Every good manager does his or her best to follow the rules placed upon them by the organization they work for.

I have written my experiences and suggestions with the hope that it would provoke thought and provide guidance to managers. Whether you agree or disagree with my observations, I maintain that the position of a line manager is significant to the success of the organization. Without line managers the civilized world would come to a standstill, whether considering the historic building of the pyramids or the more contemporary U.S. space program. It took line managers to implement the actions to accomplish these projects. Just suppose for a moment that our electrical, gas, oil, transportation, medical and food systems have incompetent managers? We often read of explosions, ships sinking, people suffering illnesses that are tied to inept managers – managers that lack in ability and courage.

Oct 1, 2014 Woodridge, Illinois, USA

WHY BE A MANAGER?

1. To take satisfaction in the conception, design, fabrication, completion and operation of a project.
2. To provide contributions that make a finer product.
3. To train people within your organization to expand their knowledge and to become better people.
4. To make more money, have more freedom and to create more time to study and learn.

I remember being a young manager married with children and their associated responsibilities. This gave me a lifetime of understanding what many of my employees were experiencing. I remember how filled my weekends were with trying to satisfy all my family needs, and how great it was on Mondays to go to work and direct others.

TRAINING

This was the core contributing factor to my peace of mind and the strength of my groups. I loved work but I also liked personal freedom. I wanted my group to function at a high level without my being there. To accomplish this I trained, trained and trained some more. The training consisted of small short classes on all aspects of our responsibilities.

I would read trade magazines, cut out articles, and pass them on to be read by employees. Employees needed to initial their review and then return the items back to me. I enabled employees to make out requisitions for items that would make our jobs easier.

As a regular practice, I wrote and had my employees review procedures for all aspects of our work. We took apart virtually every mechanical item used on our projects and discussed what made them tick. We made all practical repairs on our equipment. By doing this, not only did this develop the employees' knowledge resulting in their professional advancement, I also become more proficient. To stay ahead of the curve, I would contact managers from other operating systems similar to ours. I would visit these sites with my employees. All of these activities took time but served to bolster the groups' confidence in their abilities and also made them feel that our group was special.

SAFETY

With a high cost of medicine a manager must instruct and enforce safety. These are the reasons:

1. Should an employee injure a back, or other part of their body, it will be painful.
2. Loosing time requires others to fill in, placing a burden on the entire group.
3. The employee cannot even help out at home or with their other activities.
4. Healthcare costs increase.
5. There are absolutely no winners.

I was never refused a request for safety equipment. For example, I added hydraulic lift tail gates on our trucks to prevent back injuries. I encouraged employees to recommend equipment to prevent injuries. The only times I would lose my cool would be when an employee was breaking safety rules and possibly injuring themselves. I did my best to write procedures to eliminate any safety problems.

STARTING SALARIES FOR NEW EMPLOYEES

I was told by a boss that starting salaries are a cat and mouse game. The goal is to get the best person at the lowest cost. This may be a fine strategy for managers that don't have day to day contact with these people or have to determine the rewards for workers' contributions. It has been my experience that line management should offer a new employee maximum money for the position applied for.

Many people find this concept disturbing. Allow me to explain. Soon the new employee will find out what all his fellow employees are being paid and if he feels that there is an injustice the griping will start. If he or she doesn't measure up during his review period, the person is gone. Should they stay, sometime later each manager is allotted a fixed quantity of money for the entire group. It is the line manager's decision who gets more or less money. If a new person was hired low, and turns out to be a gem, it places pressure on the manager to compensate the new employee with extra money taking that money from the other employees in the group.

Being a good but average performer starting at a reasonable salary means politically more money for the entire group. This concept in both the short and long run benefits everyone.

NEW HIRES

1. The usual review time for a new employee is 90 days. The employee should be told of the 90 day trial period.
2. The manager should list in writing what is expected of the employee other than what is in the company handbook. Review with the new employee:
    a. Company policy
    b. Safety aspects of job
    c. Dress code
    d. Expected working hours and possible demands to work in addition to regular hours
    e. General attitude toward fellow employees
    f. Job requirements and be clear on expectations
    g. Two thirty day review periods and mark them on the calendar

DISCHARGING EMPLOYEES

I have been laid off and the method used had a profound effect on how I choose to let people go. I was told it was over on a Friday, one hour before normal working hours ended, just after completing a large money making project. The company had tons of work. At the time I'll never forget my anger! I was living pay check to pay check and my young family was just starting to clear some extra money. Since I just had completed a very successful project I examined why I had been let go.

The nation was undergoing changes in racial equality and the company was rife with bigoted people. I made a choice to live in a visible, integrated community. I never spoke of racial equality but the penalty for association was dismissal.

Removing an employee is a very serious decision. Most people have families or obligations that require a paycheck. Once it is established that the employee does not "Fit in" the group or their behavior fails to meet standards, they must go. Often the person realizes this but finds it difficult to move on. My solution is to be frank and to tell the person that there is absolutely no future within the group. That there will be no pay raises and limited responsibilities. Mark a date on the calendar and tell them to start looking for a job change (usually 30 days). Chat with the person. This has always worked for me. End their time with the group with a party and all the team members content for their fellow employee. Remember, even the worst employee has friends and how you handle a discharge will affect the morale of the entire group.

DIFFICULT PERSONNEL

My career as a manager began when I was 33 years old. I was hired as a senior technologist during a very difficult state of the project. Seventeen people were working on the enterprise project. A senior engineer was in charge of our group and a senior scientist directed all of us. Within the group was a technician that was the rudest, most difficult person that I have ever known. He would rip items from peoples' hands and call them names. He had no favorites and treated all people equally poorly.

He was also the brightest workaholic person I have ever known. By working with him I was on an unprecedented learning curve, absorbing technical knowledge and loving it. About eighteen months later I entered the work floor to find it was empty of people. Thinking I had missed a notice of a group meeting I went to the senior scientist's office. He told me that sixteen people of our group were in personnel refusing to work with this difficult technician. I was in shock that no one in the group, some of whom I knew well, had told me of their plans. They assumed I was a close friend of his and would inform on them. The senior scientist told me to go home and decide if we should transfer and replace all 16 people and keep the brilliant tech or let the tech go. It was a sad decision but the next day I told the senior scientist that sixteen people cannot be wrong and if the problem tech stayed that in time we would be back with the same situation. The difficult technician was transferred and three months later I was placed in charge of the entire remaining group.

Later in my career I was part of a larger group of over 200 people. When the director of the group had a difficult employee he would transfer that employee to me as a "Freebie." This happened many times. Most of these people were good workers having personality differences with their previous managers.

One person was a verbal bully who stood over six feet six inches and weighed about 325 pounds. I, being raised in the inner city and a war veteran, do not frighten easily. I'm only average size and weight but can pretty well handle the really bad guys or the bullies.

I sat him down and reviewed his responsibilities and within a week he went out of control. I wrote him up when no manager had ever previously written a letter of misbehavior on him. I gave him his copy and he went bunkers again! I immediately wrote a second letter for his personnel records. Three letters were a reason for dismissal or time off with no pay. What a change came over him. He soon found a new group that would have him. The power of the pen wins again!

On the other side of the coin one must be able to distinguish the bullies from a truly troubled person. A fine growing company in my area was run by a group of talented managers. The VP was a young, bright, good guy and had had it with a worker. On a Friday afternoon he fired the worker. The worker went to his locker, drew a revolver, and killed the VP. This was a severe loss for the family and business. It has been my experience that individuals with no wealth or material goods are the ones who exhibit the most erratic and strange behavior. A manager must be careful and get professional help before confronting these people.

GIFTS AND CONTRACTS

I was Field Inspector on a low bid multi-million dollar contract. The low bidder had a history of bidding low and then finding reasons to charge more and being successful in receiving additional funds upon completion of the contract. The president of the bid company would wine, dine and give gifts to people involved with each contract commitment.

To manage this company I kept two logs, one at their facility and one of my own. I took pictures and sent letters to all people involved with this contract. I would not participate in the management's usual bounties. When the contract was completed he submitted a bill for additional funds and was rejected for the first time. One cannot change certain cultures but you do not have to participate in them.

I recall being very busy on a new project. I was called upon to get a massive part completed at a very large facility. The part was 8 months behind schedule and one of our senior people had failed to get the item completed and shipped. I was really annoyed; my current job could suffer; and the plant where I needed to work to resolve the problem was in a major traffic area and it was a noisy, dirty facility. This was a real bummer.

The very first visit to the facility I was asked to wait for the company president to come into his swanky office. I waited for over two hours. When he came in I refused to shake his hand and told him that until the job was shipped I was going to be the biggest pain in the neck that he had ever dealt with. I was not going to be like the nice engineer he had been jerking around before! He called his shop foreman and told him he didn't want to see me again and to get that job out of the shop. It was shipped in three weeks. I'm basically a nice guy but it doesn't matter who or what position a person holds, don't try to take advantage of my group or the organization I represent.

A very large expensive vessel I was responsible for was delivered to our facility. Foundations were ready for the vessel. It was being placed in a tight spot and two cranes were in position to lift and set this expensive unit. Our in house rigging supervisor had contracted an outside rigging contractor. The cables from both cranes were tied to the vessel. I stopped the procedure and tried to have the leader of the rigging crew and our supervisor review the method they were using to lift the large and heavy vessel. They just "Poo-pooed" me telling me how vast their experience was. When the vessel left the ground it swung out of control striking a solid post. The damage to the vessel was to the tune of $60,000 in a matter of seconds.

There are times that one should take a few minutes and listen to people that truly care and have experience. The rigging company paid for the repair. It was not a profitable day.

My recommendations are:

1. Being cozy with contractors can have major pitfalls. Is the price worth your job or reputation?
2. Get in the habit of writing specifications. It really pays.
3. Get at least 2 bidders yet 3 are better. Change bidders often.
4. For expensive or important bids – Request a meeting with the low bidder before awarding the contract. Keep records of the meeting and have the contractor sign the notes.
5. Clarify and document that the contract people have the right to visit and take pictures of the job in progress.

CHAIN OF COMMAND

All employees like to know who's running the store. It is important to post a block diagram on how managers and the fellow workers fit into the "Chain of command." This indicates the manager is comfortable in his position and shows employees they have a position with the company.

Every six months I would invite my supervisor to speak with my subordinates (limit to ½ hour). I would always introduce him, giving his background and thanking him for taking the time to meet with us. I was not always fond of my bosses but we still needed their support and I kept up good business relationships.

BODY LANGUAGE

Body language can be infectious. It shows our emotions, excitement, disappointment, concerns, etc.

The interesting moments where knowledge of body language is useful is during difficult times such as finding solutions required to calm workers. The manager that can read one or more people's body language will find a method or means to solve the problem on hand. There are some very good books written on body language, I encourage managers to read them.

Do not underestimate the effect of the location upon the body language and the resulting impact on behavior. When I would come into a practically impossible problem I would take a coffee break away from the area. The new environment allowed my team to relax and think "Outside the box". It never failed to find a new direction and solve the problem.

STARTING AND FINISHING A JOB

A few years ago I applied for position of CEO's Assistant. The CEO was a bright, serious person. After several preliminary interviews he asked me to sit in on a senior staff meeting. The principal discussion was about a prominent piece of equipment still in the building that was overdue for delivery. The Project Manager was refusing to ship the equipment without all of his final adjustments. The CEO asked me what should he do? I told the CEO to ship the Project Manager with the equipment and bill the customer. On a side note, the CEO made a significant offer to hire me.

One time I was immersed in a multimillion dollar job with a tight completion schedule. We were waiting on approval from the Chief Program Director to begin. The paperwork sat and sat and sat. The Director had never been responsible for a project of that magnitude and it was delaying his action. Finally I had waited until we were alone and I had a chat with him assuring him that we had the ability to complete the task ahead. I would not leave until he had signed the paperwork.

The job went well and he was awarded a major promotion.

I worked for a small, growing and progressive company. I was young, and on a learning curve, so the Chief Manager was mentoring me. He offered these words of wisdom. The most difficult part of a job is starting. That an individual delays starting a project because one does not fully comprehend the full scope of the project and fearing of failure is part of the average manager's approach. Later in the life of a project the comfort level sets in and the job drags with the uncertainty for what the next job has in store.

He was right. I always requested a completion date when I assigned jobs to offset this natural tendency.

DIVISION OF RESPONSIBILITIES

Huge operations have many areas that require looking after, such as vehicles, buildings, equipment, spare parts, stock rooms, food areas, tools etc. I assigned people to these tasks; this gave me an indication of which people took pride and responsibility. Organized areas are cleaner and have reduced paperwork.

One position I took over had a large facility area and I found that the restroom was old and not very clean. I immediately changed the fixtures, painted and replaced the floor. What a morale builder it was! One of the most positive comments I received as a new manager was how glad they were that I upgraded the rest room.

SALES PERSONS

I worked for a small and growing company that had a rule that all personnel must greet and be nice to visiting sales people. The assumption was that these same sales people would speak well of our company as they visited other companies. I learned a lot from sales people and even treated some to lunch, which surprised them.

I was having a technical problem with a shaft seal and I asked a visiting salesman what was new on seals. He called the research division of his company to help and I spoke with a very knowledgeable person who recommended a particular material. I made several seals with this material that had outstanding results! That salesperson saved our organization thousands of dollars.

MANAGING RELATIONS WITH WORKERS

I recall during my first role as a manager that one of my senior techs was working on a project. Being anxious to see the job completed, I started to help. A few minutes later he disappeared and later I found him drinking coffee in our small kitchen area. He told me that if I was going to do his job then he would go and drink some coffee. After that I kept my hands in my pocket unless someone asked for help.

A manager must separate his personal life from his workers. Palling around with workers after hours and on the weekend causes dissension. I have witnessed managers crossing this line resulting in a negative effect on the morale of the group. Many times workers have asked for advice on their personal matters. My response is to tell them that there are better qualified people to provide guidance.

There are circumstances that require care and compassion when you are a manager. One example was when one of my techs had lost his only sibling, a sister to cancer. She had left behind a husband and two young children. I spoke to our group and we discussed how we could ease his pain. Another time, an employee's wife suffered a still born child. I sent him and his wife a card with my condolences. He later told me that I was the only person to do so. The one event that once really affected our group was when a very talented technician was moving to a new house with his wife and two small children. During the move his wife fell at the new house and died.   I was the first person he called. (He and his wife were only children.) I had recently buried my father so I was familiar with the required arrangements. I made all the funeral plans and his fellow technicians were the pall bearers. At that time I was a young manager of two years. It was a very trying time indeed.

GENERAL MORALITY

This is one of the more difficult areas for managers. For the happily married or happily single person, sort of the storybook individual, general morality is easier to define. But today's changing cultures and attitudes create many pitfalls for employees. I recall knowing and liking a fellow manager that held Christian bible and fellowship meetings during the lunchtime. I was chatting with a worker in his group and made a remark regarding how nice a person his manager was. His response was "Yes, if you are the kind of Christian he thinks that you should be."

I also knew a secretary who was upset by the boss' affairs and indiscretions. It caused her to lose her job.

I recall having lunch with a nice lady and someone later spread a nasty rumor that we spent noontime at a local motel. One could understand why reverend Billy Graham never allowed himself to be alone with a woman (except his wife)!

One time, when I took over a new group, the first move I made was to have all the naughty pictures removed. So many people gave me positive comments regarding this action. I tried to make work a haven away from any problems that existed in their lives.

Here are some suggestions:

1. Review the company employee manual, often. If one does not exist, write one.
2. Should you become aware of any existing bullying or teasing, put an immediate stop to it. Write up a warning to the culprits that if such behavior continues they will need to find other employment.
3. Put a stop to all blatant potty mouths.
4. Enforce a dress code.
5. Remind employees that the area they work is open to visitors and family members.

EMPLOYEE REVIEWS

Personnel departments (HR) love to draw up methods to review employees. They love to accumulate statistics and write about workers' deficiencies. They like to apply what they have been taught in school. Employees dislike reviews and some are sick for days before and after the reviews. My general experience with HR policies has been their recommendation is to say or write nine good points and one negative point about an employee for their review. I have found that the only thing employees remember is the negative comment!

People in personnel do not have to live a year with these unhappy people until their next review! I learned to deal promptly with problems or corrections in performance when they happen and not wait until review time. I gave nothing but positive reviews and many people used them to show to their mates and some used the reviews to get advanced positions. The people I reviewed were happy and stress free, not like their past supervisors' reviews.

PARTIES, HOLIDAYS AND VACATIONS

A group I managed asked if they could take a temporary intern out for lunch as a going away party. I was caught off guard, being very busy at that time, and I said "Sure" and they insisted I ride with them. Well we went to a bar about 10 miles from our work place. The bar featured ladies wearing and selling under garments. I sweated out this two hour lunch, fun for all but me. I sure learned my lesson and ask lots of questions before going to a party off site.

A 24-7 operation poses scheduling problems with vacations and holidays. I have worked for companies that shut the plant down so everyone can plan accordingly. Sometimes that option was not available and I requested a three month advance notice for one or more weeks' vacation. I filled in for my employees where there were any serious conflicts.

As a manager I was flexible with people being late, mornings and lunches, but there was a clear understanding that when I asked people to work through lunch or evenings and weekends that it was expected. Should they refuse to work they should expect serious consequences.

DRUGS AND ALCOHOL

I borrowed a person from another group occasionally. He was a special worker with a great attitude. I was told that he was caught smoking a marijuana cigarette while at lunch and was dismissed. This was too bad.

Another good worker was caught with a pinch of cocaine and was let go. I have known many employees that have had liquid lunches at the local bars and others that kept liquor bottles in their desks or lockers. Good workers can have bad habits that cause them to lose their job.

One of the people in my group told me he would not partner with a fellow worker because he was taking illicit drugs. I told him that this was a serious accusation and to say nothing to no one. I went to the head of (H.R.) Personnel for some direction. She told me I was on my own and to let her know how I handled it. Thanks a lot I thought to myself.

Since this was a medical problem I approached the organization's medical doctor and he suggested that we advance the accused's yearly medical checkup. As part of his physical he was tested for drug use and tested clean. I told the accuser that if he had an issue with this employee I would somehow drive him out of our group with a bad reference.

It turned out that the complaining employee had other issues in his life and shortly left our group. I had no further complaints about the other employee.

All companies must define their policy towards drugs and alcohol. It is beyond the average manager's capability to manage these issues and HR should assist.

MY TAKE ON DRUGS

We have a series of agencies in our Nation battling the drug problem. Although schools, towns, cities, townships, counties, states and federal government claim to work on solutions, the problem still grows. I believe that we have not shocked our children to the damage that is done to their bodies and brains by drugs. For example, when I was in the military service being shipped to Korea during the war we had to watch a film of actual troops with injuries from exposure to the cold. The film showed gruesome blackened toes, fingers, ears and noses being removed with pliers. I was shocked into awareness and that winter when I served in the field I kept myself protected. I still see the images of fellow soldiers in that film.

Young people like their bodies and if they were exposed to the truth of their peers lying dead with all of the sores, needle marks and blemishes caused by drugs, there will be a reaction and awareness that is not there today. I'm sure that many parents would object to showing the truth, but the results would be worth it.

COMPENSATION

1. Early in my working career I belonged to several major labor unions. They offered safer working conditions, cost of living increases and seniority protection. All of this was a comfort level with modest gains to Middle American life style. Since the demise of unions, workers have sought to recover the same level of benefits from current employers.

2. I have been elected and served on a public board. Our recent government officials at all levels have demonstrated that they cannot control pension plans. All forms of public government pensions must be discontinued. There are many private plans these people can join. The inability of the average taxpayer to pay for these pensions is drowning their finances. Europe's pension plans virtually broke the budgets of most nations.

3. Elected official incumbents have treasure chests accumulated after terms in office. They are large enough to discourage good people from entering the race. I would make a law specifying that all citizens holding or

running for office must spend all monies to their campaign or donate the balance to a charity within 30 days of the election. There should also be a limit on the amount of personal money that can be used (such as $0.25 per person with the district.)

RACE, SEX & the SEXES

Being a country that's so diverse, with laws that are provided to protect rights of all citizens, we need to understand that we humans are not perfect. On occasions we make and say inappropriate remarks or tactless mistakes. Personnel departments have small gray areas for such occasions. Line managers need to have larger, within limits, grey areas.

There may be times that valuable workers are in hot water for slighting a sensitive person. Dismissing this individual could have a real negative effect on operations or morale. I was faced with this situation on multiple occasions. Once, a manager from another large group was making unsavory remarks to a temporary black worker within my control. I liked this manager but I told him that one more remark and I would write him up, with him knowing that documenting such remarks would lead to termination. The problem ceased.

Another time an openly declared gay person accused just about everyone of being discriminatory towards gays, including me. The way he spun events made my head spin, presenting difficult situations. The problem resolved itself when he, unfortunately, became ill and left our organization. Potential discrimination events really press managers to address issues and be fair to all people.

One day my supervisor called and informed me that one of our best workers was accused of groping a lady in another group. I immediately called in my worker who admitted to the incident. I knew the lady and had helped her with several projects. I told this person, a ranking craftsman, to go to the victim, apologize and ask the lady to forgive him as a favor to me. She said that she would. I had almost lost an experienced worker. I did tell him that there would not be a second chance!

There are times that a manager has no immediate and obvious solution and a good experienced manager has to calm the situation. It is best to remind workers that our nation is special because we respect the rights of all people. In the event of a serious personnel problem, if possible, take a day to cool off before resolving the circumstances.

FOREIGN OPPORTUNITIES FOR MANAGERS

Foreign companies, particularly those in the Far East, have problems in the field interacting with other companies (in particular Latin and South American companies.) Culture work ethics and other workplace behavior cause delays and difficulties in completing projects. USA managers, because of our blend of cultures, are in demand. The world is a welcoming place for competent, adventurous USA managers.

ENERGY AND ENVIRONMENT

Energy and water will dominate the world economies now and for years to come. Managers should make their workers aware of these costs. These costs affect all aspects of a company – profits, stock price, employee jobs and salaries.

Managers should know the basic science of energy, watts, kilowatts, BTU's, cubic feet, etc. A manager should teach, or have a person give a short introduction to, the basics of energy and water that affect costs at work and at home. I was responsible for a huge compressor system that had water valves operated by an old fashioned temperature bulb. I changed the valves to electric, operated by sensitive electronic feedback, and this saved the electric bill $100,000 a year ($1M in 10 years!). Many times a weak manager will take the easy solution, of high energy cost, rather than research or introducing more efficient methods. Employees should be encouraged to suggest methods that would reduce energy costs.

INFORMATION AGE

The internet age is here and in just a touch of our fingers we can obtain and learn most anything about anything and everything recorded since civilization began.

There are only so many hours in a day and one needs to be prudent on how one spends that time. Like any tool, are we the master of it or is it the master of us? A wise manager must have discipline as the web is just like junk mail, and a person is easily distracted by clever peddlers. Smarter managers are not drawn in and advise their workers that those who get caught up in internet distractions will be delaying any advancement.

VEHICLES

Vehicles of all types are used in all industries. They can be an expensive part of a budget!

No matter who drives a vehicle someone should be assigned the accountability, such as mileage, condition, cleanness, fuel usage etc. Vehicles represent the Company. For example, how often do we see vehicle engines idling, spending expensive fuel? Usually this happens when no one was answerable.

WHEN TO TAKE A STAND

In my life I have known and met some of the finest people who are managers. I have had the privilege to have spent time with a police chief, minister, YMCA Director, Mayor, people holding public office and NCO's in the military service. These people are making our time within our local communities and our nation a more pleasant one. My children are well educated and caring due to a large part because of the public education they received.

There may arise on a rare occasion a situation when one must bring to attention to another group or manager a serious situation that needs to be corrected. I have done this three times in my managerial career. On each occasion it was related to a safety issue. Each time I was admonished for my bringing it to their attention and I have no regrets for doing so. Just remember "You don't expect a pat on the back." I always went through the proper chain of command. When safety, product reliability, or company reputation is at risk, and your immediate supervisor rejects your suggestion or refuses to move on the serious problem, I do not hesitate to inform the top officials or company board members. There may be consequences but one will sleep better.

COMMUNITY RESPONSIBILITY

Having input or a voice with our federal government is a tall order. State and country governments are a little easier, but participating in local government can easily have beneficial results. My children told me when companies or parents spoke to their classes it was very interesting. Companies should encourage employees to participate and have programs contributing time and fund drives.

I think a system giving businesses tax breaks for every employee hired that lives within the local tax borders would benefit the company, employee and other local businesses.

THE MANAGER'S WORLD

All my suggestion and experiences are written to assist in making a new manager's job less stressful, more enjoyable and productive. Work dominates our life so let's make it a great ride as we will surely get old and want to remember an interesting journey.

We gave it our best shot, made a nice salary, met and dealt with interesting people. I still get calls from fine workers that are now supervisors; love of family, life and job. What else could one expect?

IN CONCLUSION

For me, being a front line manager was a very special job. From creation to implementation, at times with state of the art products, the job was always interesting and enjoyable. The improvements and cost savings that I made on the systems easily covered all my salary while I worked there. I have been elected and served in local government for 12 years, been a board member of a 90 million dollar credit union and ran for political office many times. Good managers that I have met during these endeavors have been very interesting. Managers can be a cut above the average person.

Teddy Roosevelt is one of my favorite presidents and his address about being in the arena with reward and disappointments but quite a ride, are true to form. Framed and hanging on my office wall are two of my favorite proverbs.

"People are like tea bags, you don't know their strengths until they are in hot water." *Unknown author*

"The credit belongs to the man who is actually in the arena – whose face is marred by dust and sweat and blood…who knows the great enthusiasms, the great devotions – and spends himself in a worthy cause – who at best if he wins knows the thrills of high achievement – and if he fails at least fails while daring greatly- so that his place shall never be with those cold and timid souls who know neither victory nor defeat." *Theodore Roosevelt*

I have read many management books but do not remember any discussing actual situations in a manager's life. I hope all that is written will stimulate thought and provoke discussion.

THE AUTHOR

Carl B. Pallaver was a first generation American, the product of emigrant parents from the Dolomite mountain area of Austria, now part of northern Italy. Both parents had only a basic primary education.

Speaking no English, Carl started school in a coal mining town. These humble beginnings provide the author with compassion for all new immigrants to our nation.

His early childhood was spent playing in abandoned coal mines, sulfur creeks and flying kites. At the age of eight his parents moved to a large city and a working class neighborhood. Education was not a high priority to his parents. Carl signed his own report cards and began working part-time at the age of twelve and graduated high school at the age of sixteen. He found working full time to be a "breather" from school. Family circumstances made him live on his own at the age of eighteen.

Carl's next sixteen years included over 15 different employers, night school with technical subjects and a wide range of technical jobs. This background made him a special candidate for the challenging work at three major advanced research institutions. During this period of his life he was happily married, blessed with three well educated, independent children.

Carl has served in the military, held public office and has served on the board of a large credit union. He has had a very interesting and rewarding life.

Appendix A – SAMPLE TEST FOR GENERAL TECHNICAL TECHNICIANS

When hiring a new employee there may be several candidates. A method I used that assisted me in making a decision was a short test. My only request was that the candidate not guess on an answer. Some of my best new hires were determined by the outcome of these tests. Included are two sample tests.

Circle the correct answer (please do not guess)

1. Which is inert gas?
   a. Hydrogen
   b. Oxygen
   c. Nitrogen
2. 50/50 solder melts at what temperature?
   a. 150 degrees F
   b. 450 degrees F
   c. 800 degrees F
3. Pipe threads have:
   a. More threads
   b. Deeper threads
   c. An angle
4. Which is the finer finish:
   a. 32
   b. 64

c. 128

5. Which is the easiest to weld
   a. Cast iron
   b. Aluminum
   c. Steel

6. A 4 inch square has 10 PSI of pressure on it. The total pressure is:
   a. 40 PSI
   b. 80 PSI
   c. 160 PSI

7. Which plastic can take a higher temperature?
   a. Plexiglass
   b. Teflon
   c. Polyethylene

8. Which is a better insulator?
   a. Paper matt
   b. Glass matt
   c. Vacuum

9. Which voltage is more dangerous?
   a. 120 volts
   b. 240 volts
   c. 480 volts

10. Part of the efficiency of a standard induction motor depends on:
    a. Speed
    b. Torque
    c. Air gap

Answers to General Tech Questions.

1. C
2. B
3. C
4. A
5. C
6. C
7. B
8. C
9. All
10. C

Appendix B – SAMPLE TEST FOR ELECTRONIC TECHNICIANS – Low voltage (<100V)

1. What color are wire jackets for USB cable's differential data lines (D+ and D-)?

a) green and white

b) white with green stripes, and green with white stripes

c) black and red

d) yellow and red

2. Which cable size has the largest diameter?

a) 18AWG

b) 24AWG

c) 32AWG

3. What is the melting point of Sn-Pb eutectic solder?

a. 212 degrees F

b. 361 degrees F

c. 460 degrees F

d. 801 degrees F

4. Why is PPE important?

a. Critical to ensuring quality systems meet ISO9001 requirements

b. Critical to ensuring import/export regulations are adhered to

c. Critical to ensuring devices meet UL safety regulations

d. Critical to ensuring employee safety

5. What is the key advantage of using Polyswitch resettable fuses?

a. Wider hysteresis curve

b. No need to replace tripped fuse

c. Faster trip time

d. Extremely high current rating

6. Which of the following is not a way to measure electrical current?

a. Galvanometer

b. Clamp probe to multimeter or oscilloscope

c. Voltmeter across a shunt resistor

d. Direct current mirror

7. What is the nominal rms voltage and frequency of residential/commercial mains AC power in the USA?

a. 120V/50Hz

b. 120V/60Hz

c. 230V/50Hz

d. 230V/60Hz

8. What is the peak-to-peak voltage of residential/commercial mains AC power in the USA?

a. 336V

b. 336A

c. 644V

d. 644A

9. Which of the following passive electrical components have polarity?

a. Resistor

b. Inductor

c. Ceramic capacitor

d. Electrolytic capacitor

10. Which of the following passive electrical components do NOT have polarity?

a. LED

b. Diode

c. Fuse

d. Electrolytic capacitor

11. What happens if a polarized component is installed backwards?

a. Destroys component

b. Reverses the voltage across the component

c. Reverses the current across the component

12. Which if the following is NOT a common method of preventing ESD damage to devices?

a. Controlling humidity of room

b. Controlling temperature of room

c. Use static dissipative packaging, flooring, furniture, and clothing

d. Connected ESD straps for all human handlers

13. You want to power a motor whose specifications are: output power of 100W, power factor of 0.8. How much power does your power supply need to provide?

a. 80 W

b. 100 W

c. 125 W

d. 800 W

Question	Answer	Comments
1	A	USB is the dominant peripheral connection interface for all consumer electronics. Or at least it was for the last 15 years. This shows that they've worked with USB, created cabling for it.
2	A	Simple, need to understand they know AWG scale.
3	B	Will show they understand a bit about solder, what temperature it melts at, what temp to set their soldering gun. Also interesting to note that as electronics industry moves away from leaded solder, the most commonly used SnAg & SnAgCu solders melt around 460.
4	D	PPE is widely used industry term, it stands for "Personal Protective Equipment". It refers mostly to protective glasses, but can include hats, gloves, coats, boots. The question is designed to see if the tech has any familiarity with safety systems &

		terminology.
5	B	Just checking what familiarity they have with fuse components
6	D	Seeing what they know about measurement techniques
7	B	Seeing if they have basic familiarity with AC power
8	A	Seeing if they understand the relationship between rms and peak
9	D	Checking their understanding of various components' polarity
10	C	Checking their understanding of various components' polarity
11	A	Checking if they've ever lit up a capacitor
12	B	Checking if they understand how to mitigate ESD issues
13	C	Checking basic understanding of AC power systems, of true power vs apparent power.